P9-BZZ-337

MACHINE EMBROIDERY
and *More*

10 STEP-BY-STEP PROJECTS USING BORDER FABRICS AND BEADS

KRISTEN DIBBS

C&T PUBLISHING

For Richard and Phillip

© 2001 Kristen Dibbs

Editor: Beate Marie Nellemann
Technical Editors: Peggy Strawhorn Kass and Joyce Engels Lytle
Copy Editor: Stacy Chamness
Cover Designer: Christina D. Jarumay
Design Director/Book Designer: Christina D. Jarumay
Illustrator: Phillip Dibbs
Production Assistants: Kirstie L. McCormick and Jeffery Carrillo
Photographers: Andy Payne and Oliver Ford. Photo on page 34 by Steven Buckley, Photographic Reflections.
Stylist: Kathy Tripp
Published by C&T Publishing, Inc., P.O. Box 1456 Lafayette, California 94549

All rights reserved. No part of this work covered by the copyright hereon may be reproduced and used in any form or any means—graphic, electronic, or mechanical, including photocopying, recording, taping, or information storage and retrieval systems—without written permission of the publisher.

Exception: Publisher and author give permission to photocopy a maximum of two copies of page 39, for personal use only.

Attention Teachers: C&T Publishing, Inc. encourages you to use this book as a text for teaching. Contact us at 1-800-284-1114 or www.ctpub.com for more information about the C&T Teachers Program.

We take great care to ensure that the information included in this book is accurate and presented in good faith, but no warranty is provided nor results guaranteed. Since we have no control over the choices of materials or procedures used, neither the author nor C&T Publishing, Inc. shall have any liability to any person or entity with respect to any loss or damage caused directly or indirectly by the information contained in this book.

Trademarked (™) and Registered Trademark (®) names are used throughout this book; rather than use the symbols with every occurrence of a trademark and registered trademark name, we are using the names only in the editorial fashion and to the benefit of the owner, with no intention of infringement.

Library of Congress Cataloging-in-Publication Data
Dibbs, Kristen
   Machine embroidery and more : 10 step-by-step projects using border fabrics and beads / Kristen Dibbs.
     p. cm.
   ISBN 1-57120-162-9
   1. Embroidery, Machine--Patterns. 2. Beadwork--Patterns.   I. Title.
TT772 .D53 2000
746.44'028--dc21
                            2001001136

Printed in China
10 9 8 7 6 5 4 3 2 1

Acknowledgments

This book has grown like a friendship quilt, with individual contributions from some special people:

Karen Fail, who introduced me to the wonderful world of Quilting, and who has proven a tireless, knowledgeable, and kind friend every step of the way.

Diane Rose, who quilted two of my quilts for me, and taught me so much.

Davana Kalliffay, for assistance with beading and hand sewing.

Andy Payne and Oliver Ford for their wonderful photography.

Kathy Tripp, for her elegant styling.

Richard Dibbs, my husband, whose loving support, attention to detail, and excellent organizational skills are the stitches that hold me together.

Phillip Dibbs, my son, who spent countless hours patiently designing my diagrams and illustrations exactly the way I wanted them.

My special thanks to the following companies for their generous support with fabrics, threads, and products used for projects in the book.

Sulky of America
Hobbs Bonded Fibres
RJR Fabrics
Robert Kaufman Fabrics
Benartex Fabrics®
Quilters Only/Springs Industries®
XLN Fabrics, Sydney Australia
HobbySew, Sydney, Australia®

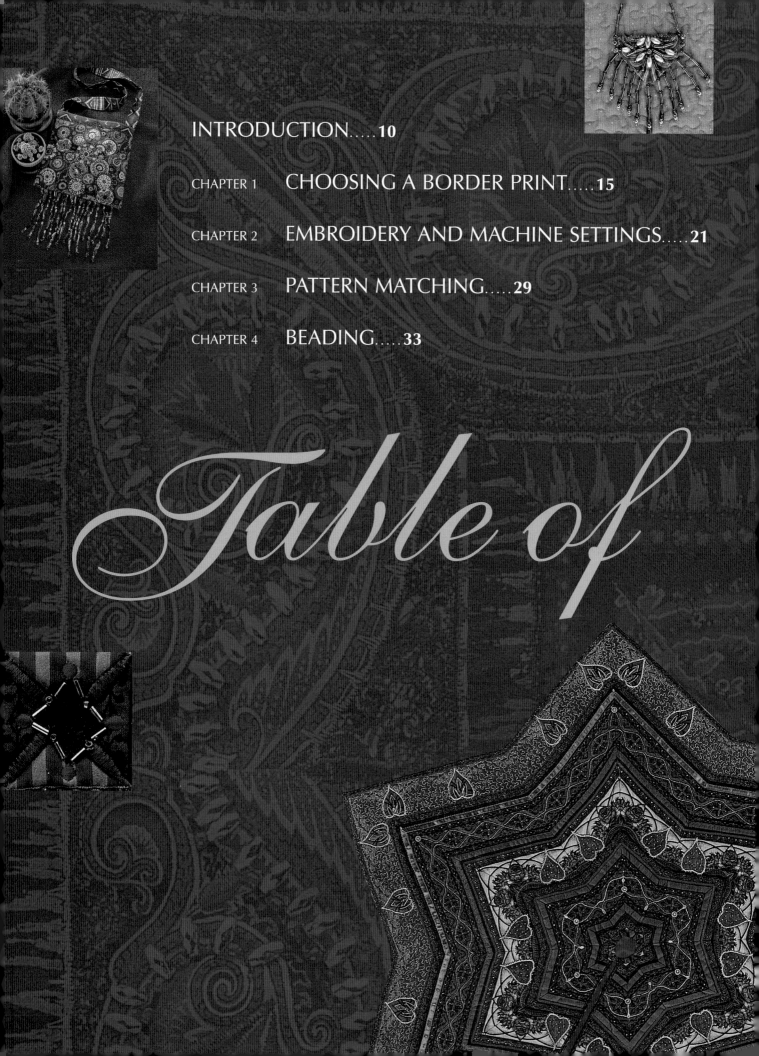

Table of

CHAPTER 5 PROJECTS

Contents

Introduction

Once upon a time, before I became involved with textile arts, a border was just a border, something that went around the edge of a quilt or a picture. In 1986, when I first became enthralled with my new passion for machine embroidery, I always selected plain fabrics, all the better to show off my stitching. In 1998, I made my first visit to the USA, including the International Quilt Festival in Houston. Never had I seen such an enormous and bewildering range of quilts, fabrics, notions, and awesome skill in combining so many different elements. I was inspired to go home and bravely try my hand at quilting, putting together some of the ideas that fascinated me on that first wonderful trip.

My contact with quilting up to that time had been minimal. Math was something that terrified me early and often in my childhood, and as an adult I would steer very clear of anything that looked as if it might involve measuring, hard sums, and precision. I was an artist, and the sewing machine was my drawing board. Figuring out yardage and matching points was definitely not for me.

I had seen some wonderful fabrics and some dazzling quilts at the International Quilt Festival in Houston. But I needed more. Color and texture have always been my favorite elements, and most of the quilts I saw were beautifully smooth, flat, and perhaps—dare I say it—just a little, well, plain? Someone once said, "Too much surface decoration is barely enough," and I guess this comment started me on a journey of discovery. I began to look at quilt fabrics in a totally new way, paying attention to patterns, which lent themselves to further ornamentation. Oriental and Indian designs, like paisleys, have always been my passion, and I began playing with these. What fun it was to add more and more ornamentation to those wonderful swirling curves and sinuous shapes.

Turquoise stripe block detail

The basic blue paisley fabric has been brightened with the addition of a sharp turquoise and blue stripe.

Black and gold block detail

The brilliant black and gold pineapple fabric has been partly overlaid with sheer black organza that dims the background a little, and makes the embroidery more prominent.

Blue and red block detail

This is the same blue paisley fabric as in the turquoise stripe block on page 10. However, green tulle has been used to overlay the block, slightly changing the color scheme, while still allowing the fabric design to show through.

Navy and red block

This block was one of my first blocks. The paisley fabric
has been completely covered with navy organza and
a plain blue cotton in the center square. The block is
embroidered so intensively that hardly any of the
base fabric is visible.

Cream and pearl block

This lovely scroll fabric lends itself to endless variations. An overlay of cream tulle adds a subtle textural change, and the matte surface of the fabric is highlighted with glossy rayon thread and glass pearl beads.

My first miniature quilts—little 12" squares—were made purely to amuse myself. I experimented with printed fabrics as a basis for further embellishments. Just joining pieces together was never enough for me.

I wanted more of the "fun stuff"—adding embroidery, changing the colors subtly with sheer fabrics on top, and then relaxing at night surrounded by a glittering array of beads, guilt and calorie-free, "candy for the soul." I loved the contrast between the flat, matte surface of the quilt cotton, and the shiny glitter of the glass and metallic beads. About three months later, after making my first dozen little experimental squares, I was hooked, and traveling down an exciting new pathway.

CHAPTER 1

Choosing a Border Print

*W*hen I first looked closely at the huge range of fabrics available to quilters, I discovered that there were many kinds of border print stripe fabrics and the difference revolved around the axis of symmetry. I remember learning in elementary school that the axis of symmetry is a line drawn down the center of a shape, dividing it into two identical, mirror image shapes. When you choose a border fabric for your project it is important to know what kind of border will best suit your needs.

Vertical axis of symmetry

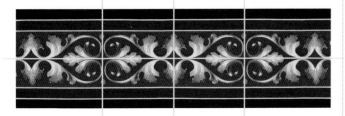

Vertical and horizontal axes of symmetry

If you want to make mitered corners with mirror image symmetry, you will need a border with a vertical axis of symmetry, such as the paisley border used in the Vest on page 64. You can also choose fabric with both a vertical and a horizontal axis of symmetry, such as the Perennial Garden border shown on the front of the Jacket project on page 70.

Border print with both a left and right directional pattern

Some borders have both a left handed and right handed repeat, on different sides of the fabric, such as the paisley pattern used in the Paisley Quilt project on page 86. These repeats can be used to form mitered corners, by using mirror image triangles, as described in that project.

Border with single direction motif

If you have a border with motifs traveling in one direction only, you may still be able to cut a 45° mitered corner, as shown with the angel border in the Christmas Angel Table Runner project on page 44.

Single direction border with a 45° mitered corner

Single direction border, no axis of symmetry

You may also decide to use a simple square corner, as shown in the Frog and Lizard Quilt project on page 53, or perhaps you want to add squares or triangles of contrast fabrics inserted at the corners.

The Frog and Lizard Quilt

Border print, no axis of symmetry

Some larger border patterns, such as the Berry Patch fabric used in the Heart Cushion project on page 38, have no axis of symmetry, and uses a large repeat motif. I used this motif as a single unit, cut into a heart shape, and appliquéd it onto a coordinating background.

All over print, no axis of symmetry

Embellishments need not be confined to border fabrics. When I saw this wonderful Native American basket fabric, I couldn't wait to add embroidery and beads to make a wonderfully complex, rich surface. See Tote Bag project, page 81.

 # Yardage

Quantities given for the projects in this book are approximate. The quantity of fabric depends, to a large extent, on the article you are making, as well as the kind of repeat pattern on the fabric you choose. If your fabric has a large repeat, such as the paisley shown in the Paisley Quilt project on page 86, it will require left- and right-hand triangles to create the mitered corners. This will require more yardage than a fabric with a smaller, simpler repeat, such as that used in the Picture Frame project on page 48. If the template you choose is an unusual shape, such as the triangle used in the Christmas Tree Skirt project on page 75, you may have sufficient fabric left over to make a second project, using the shapes left after cutting out the first set of right-and left-hand triangles required to make one skirt. So, buy more fabric than the bare minimum, to allow yourself some extra for samples and experimentation.

Overlay with Transparent Fabrics

You can be selective with your base fabric, and change all or part of the color scheme with transparent overlay fabric. You can also use the overlay to blend the color scheme of your border fabric with other plain fabrics you may choose.

Transparent overlay

Any fabric that is sheer enough to allow the printed design to show through can be used. Try tulle, organdie, organza, or even some fine laces, in one or more layers of the same or a different color. The overlay may cover all or part of your design, allowing subtle variations in tone. If you plan to enhance your design by cutting away part of the sheer overlay fabric, stitch around the edge of the shape first using a tiny, narrow zigzag stitch. This will later be covered by decorative stitching after the sheer fabric is trimmed. This technique is shown in detail in the Vest project on page 66.

Materials and Equipment

You need some basic equipment and materials to create the projects in this book, and to begin experimenting with border patterns. In addition to your usual sewing supplies, you need the following items:

Cutting mat—the bigger the better!

Fabric adhesive spray—Sulky KK 2000™ is a temporary adhesive that can be sprayed onto the wrong side of the fabric, so the pieces can be finger pressed into position, or re-positioned if required. The adhesive disappears from the fabric after a few days.

Fabric stabilizers—have a selection of stabilizers on hand, such as tear-away in heavy and light weights.

Fusible batting—fusible quilt batting in two weights, from light to firm. There are different brands on the market, such as Quilters Fusible Batting™ from June Tailor, and Gold Fuse™ from Mountain Mist®. One or two layers can be fused at the same time.

Machine embroidery hoop—approximately 9" in diameter. Buy the best quality wooden hoop you can afford, since cheap bamboo hoops don't last long and are difficult to work with.

Machine embroidery needles—these are made specially to cope with the fine rayon and metallic threads you use for embroidery. Choose size $80/12$ or $90/14$.

Marker—for drawing on the template material

Mirrors—you will need at least one rectangular or square mirror, with no frame, or you can use mirror tiles. If you have two mirrors, you can join them together with sturdy tape, so they can be opened up like a book to stand on your fabric. Mirror tiles can be bought in most hardware stores.

Permanent marking pencils—light and dark

Protractor—use the protractor to accurately measure angles when drawing unusually shaped triangles.

Quilter's rulers—large 6" x 24" ruler and triangle ruler with 90° and 45° angles for cutting accurate mitered corners 30°, 60°, and 90°.

Rotary cutter—choose the one that works best for you.

SEWING MACHINE FEET—the basic feet you need are:

Patchwork foot—with ¼" seam markings for accurate seams.

Satin stitch foot—sometimes called embroidery foot, with a wide channel underneath to ride smoothly over the raised stitching. These are also available as an open toe foot, with the central bar removed, so you can see exactly where your needle is entering the fabric.

Free motion embroidery foot—this is necessary for any free-motion work, such as filling background or outlining shapes. Depending on the brand of machine you have, you may also need a cover plate for the feed dogs, if they can't be lowered. Check with your machine supplier. I use a free-motion foot shaped like a horseshoe, with an open front. You may be able to modify the front of your free-motion foot, as the open front provides much greater visibility, therefore better accuracy for your embroidery.

Templates—you need to be able to see through your template. I use plastic template material for accurate placement on the fabric.

THREADS—**rayon** and **metallic** embroidery threads. These add a wonderful luster to your work. Machine embroidery can also be done with other embroidery threads, such as silk finish cotton, polyester, and cotton embroidery thread, which have a matte appearance.

Polyester threads—for bobbin and construction. Generally, try to match the tone of the bobbin thread to the tone of the top thread. That is, dark colors with dark colors and light colors with light colors. For special effects, or if the back of the embroidery will show, you may wish to match the color of the bobbin thread exactly to the top thread.

Beading Materials

Beading needles—for hand beading projects I use size 10 straw needles. They are also called milliner's needles. If your beading needles have very tiny eyes, you may also find a fine needle threader useful.

Beading thimble—sewing thousands of beads can be as hard on the fingers as quilting. I am indebted to my friend Davana Kalliffay for introducing me to a low cost, comfortable beading thimble—the fingers cut from triple layer rubber gloves! These are long enough to stay on comfortably, and flexible enough to allow you to feel the fabric. I wear two, on my third and fourth finger, and now I bead in comfort.

Beading tray—make one easily by attaching a piece of dark colored felt to a small tray or box lid with a low rim.

Beading thread—I use a double strand of good polyester thread, Metrosene, to attach the beads. I match the color to the background fabric.

Beads on the Vest project, page 64

CHAPTER 2

Embroidery and Machine Settings

*A*dding embroidery to the printed surface of your fabric creates another dimension. With a layer of quilt batting fused to the back of the fabric, the decorative stitching will sink down into the fabric, throwing the unstitched areas into relief. The shine of silky rayon and metallic threads provides a rich contrast to the matte surface of the cotton fabric. Choose a line on the printed fabric, and follow that with the embroidery pattern of your choice. Embroidery can be free-motion, or an automatic pattern stitch, whichever you choose.

Securing the Threads

You will change colors often during the course of each project so it is important that you secure the thread ends at the beginning and end of each color area. This can be done in one of three ways.

1. Take a few tiny backstitches, with a very short stitch length. Snip thread ends, close to fabric.

2. Leave 6" thread tails, and take these to the back of the work and darn them in by hand.

3. If sewing by hand, take tiny backstitches and finish off the thread on the wrong side. A tiny dot of a fray-stopping liquid, applied on the wrong side of the fabric, can also secure the thread so it doesn't unravel.

Stabilizing Your Embroidery

Intensive machine embroidery will often distort the base fabric. This can be avoided in the following ways.

Tear-Away Stabilizer

Use a stabilizer behind the areas to be embroidered. Fusible tear-away stabilizers are easy to use, and come in different weights. The papery finish will tear away crisply from embroidery stitches that are close together, like satin stitch. However, they tear away less easily from more widely spaced stitching, such as zigzag scribble, and more open patterns, where the stitches are not spaced closely together. This may make the work undesirably stiff, unless you are prepared to spend time removing the entire excess stabilizer with tweezers.

Fusible Quilt Batting

If you prefer a more quilted appearance, fuse one or more layers of light quilt batting to the back of the fabric. This will also act as a stabilizer.

Machine Embroidery Hoop

Intensively embroidered areas, such as those filled in with scribble stitch, should be supported by being stretched in a hoop or by using extra-firm weight stabilizer. Otherwise, the closely packed stitching may distort the fabric. Make up a selection of small quilt sandwiches and try out different techniques.

Covering Raw Edges in Appliqué

If you are adding decorative stitching to cover the raw edges of trimmed overlay fabric, select a stitch with sufficient width to cover the edge to prevent fraying. This could be a satin stitch, or a pattern stitch based on satin stitch, or even a combination of stitches, such as a honeycomb stitch, with a scallop around the edge. Have fun experimenting with the various pattern stitches on a sample swatch, until you find one that best suits your purpose.

Selecting a Pattern Stitch

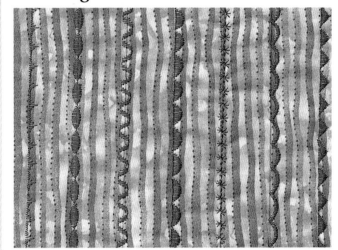

Various simple pattern stitches

The stitches you select can either be decorative such as the honeycomb stitch and the serpentine stitch, or they can be utility stitches, such as simulated overlock stitches. These are basic stitches on all modern sewing machines.

For maximum impact, select a pattern that will be visible when the article is viewed from a distance. Satin stitch patterns usually provide the most contrast. If you want your pattern stitches to flow evenly around your design, select a pattern with a fairly short pattern unit. Do a few trial samples, on a sample quilt sandwich, using the same fabric, and see how your pattern fits into the length of the line you wish to sew. Most machines have pattern adjustment controls that can lengthen or shorten a pattern a little, allowing you to fit in complete pattern units. Make a note of the length of the pattern unit on your test piece and measure the spacing of the patterns on your main fabric. You'll be able to tell whether you will need to push or pull the fabric slightly to adjust the spacing so that the pattern units fit. A slight variation in the length of individual patterns will not be noticeable. A symmetrical pattern, such as a row of triangles or a small flower or leaf, is a good guide for spacing beads.

Single Pattern Units

Single pattern units

Most modern machines also have a single pattern unit function, so you can program your machine to sew just one little heart or leaf shape, and you can then place these wherever you want them on your fabric. For longer shapes, use a tapered satin stitch, or program your machine to extend the length of the pattern unit. Make sure you always secure your threads at the beginning and end of each individual pattern unit so there will be no chance of your threads unraveling.

Free-Motion Embroidery

You may prefer the more casual charm of free-motion embroidery, where the line is drawn onto the fabric in much the same way, as you would use a pencil. Free-motion lines can be sewn with straight stitch for a fine outline, or select a narrow zigzag for a stronger line. Run the machine fast, and remember to move the fabric more slowly, to allow the zigzag stitches to lie close together.

Background Filling

Free-motion filling using a straight stitch in a stipple movement

Free-motion background filling using a small zigzag stitch in a scribble motion

You can change the dimension and color in an area of the design with background filling. This refers to the technique of stitching over the background to flatten it, thereby providing a contrast to the main raised parts of the design. Most background filling stitches are done with free-motion embroidery that allows you to get into all the little shapes and spaces. For small or intricate areas, use a straight stitch or very narrow zigzag. Larger areas can be filled with a larger zigzag or bigger circles of free-motion scribble stitch.

Free motion cable stitch

Cable stitch free-motion filling using a thicker decorative thread in the bobbin, worked with the wrong side of the fabric facing up. First outline the design from the right side.

Completed cable stitch background filling—wrong side

Cable stitch is worked from the wrong side of the fabric, so the area to be filled should first be outlined from the right side, using a straight stitch. The filling stitch can vary in density, depending on whether you want to cover the background color completely, or allow it to show through the embroidery. Stretch the fabric in a machine embroidery hoop to make it easy to move around the machine. Leave 6" tails of the threads at each end of the embroidery, and use a hand needle to pull these ends through and run them under several stitches to secure and tie off the threads.

Machine Threads

Machine embroidery threads and braid

Sulky machine embroidery rayon and metallic threads are used for the projects in this book. For the bobbin, I use a matching thread in polyester. Polyester threads in matching colors or invisible nylon thread were used for the quilting.

Machine Tension

When using rayon or metallic threads through the needle some adjustment of the top tension will usually be necessary to cope with the finer threads, which are not as strong as the regular sewing threads used for garment construction. As a general rule, loosen the top tension a little for rayon threads and loosen it further for metallic threads. As the stitch width increases, the tension also needs to be loosened, so the general rules are:

• the lighter the weight of the top thread, the looser the top tension needs to be.
• the wider the stitch width, the looser the top tension needs to be.

Due to the differences in sewing machines it is important that you experiment to find the best settings for your machine.

If you are doing both—using lightweight thread and a wide stitch—you must loosen a little for each. The wide stitch pulls more thread down through the needle; therefore the thread needs to run more loosely, which means looser top tension. Therefore, a straight stitch with a rayon or metallic thread requires the top tension to be loosened a little, and a wide satin stitch with the same thread requires it to be loosened a few degrees more. The bobbin thread should not show, and the top thread should sew smoothly without breaking. Always run a line of the test stitching before starting on your project.

Stitch Width

Many modern machines are capable of stitch widths up to 9. When using a wider stitch width for some patterns, always do a test swatch first to make sure that there will be no fabric distortion with the wider stitch widths. You may need to use an extra layer of stabilizer behind your fabric to make sure the embroidery stays flat and does not crinkle the fabric.

Machine Needles

When working with rayon and metallic embroidery threads, select a suitable needle designed to cope with these finer threads. I prefer to use a size $80/12$ or $90/14$ embroidery needle for most of my embroidery work.

Machine Settings

There are several basic settings for your machine referred to during the various projects in the book. For easy reference they are listed in the charts. Consult your own machine manual for precise directions for your machine.

Basic Straight or Zigzag Setting

Use this setting for most lines of straight stitching and some decorative utility stitches, such as honeycomb stitch and serpentine stitch.

Machine foot	Zigzag
Top thread	Rayon or metallic
Top tension	Loosened slightly
Bobbin thread	Polyester to match top thread
Bobbin tension	Normal
Feed dogs	Raised
Stitch pattern	Straight, zigzag
Stitch length	2-3
Stitch width	0-5

Basic Free-Motion Setting

Use this setting for free-motion drawing around shapes or for various kinds of background fillings. Different brands of machines have different settings for free motion stitching. Consult your machine manual for precise details.

Machine foot	Free motion embroidery foot
Top thread	Rayon or metallic
Top tension	Loosened slightly to moderately
Bobbin thread	Polyester, matching top thread
Bobbin tension	Normal
Feed dogs	Lowered or covered
Stitch pattern	Straight to zigzag
Stitch length	0
Stitch width	0-5

Stipple or Scribble?

"Stipple" is a continuous curving stitch that does not overlap. "Scribble" is tightly overlapping circles that completely fill an area and flatten it.

Basic Satin Stitch Setting

Use this setting for most automatic stitch patterns based on satin stitch, tapered satin stitch shapes, and individual pattern units.

Machine foot	Open toe or satin stitch foot
Top thread	Embroidery rayon or metallic
Top tension	Loosened several degrees
Bobbin thread	Polyester, matching top thread
Bobbin tension	Normal
Feed dogs	Raised
Stitch pattern	Automatic
Stitch length	Approximately 0.5
Stitch width	0-5

Cable Stitch Setting

When using this setting with a thicker decorative thread in the bobbin, work with the wrong side of the fabric face up. Loosen the bobbin tension until a bobbin of regular polyester thread runs freely. Then insert the bobbin of decorative thread, which will run more slowly as it is thicker. Always make a test swatch first to check your setting, and tighten the bobbin tension if the thread is running too loosely or bunching up underneath. Cable stitch can be worked with the feed dogs raised or lowered, in a straight or automatic pattern stitch, or free-motion. Both settings are given on page 27.

Cable stitch is worked with the wrong side of the fabric uppermost so the thicker thread from the bobbin will appear on the right side of the fabric. You may have to stitch guidelines first. From the right side, using a straight stitch and matching colored thread, follow the design lines on the printed fabric.

Transferring the Design with Regular Straight Stitching

Machine foot	Open toe or zigzag
Top thread	Polyester to match fabric or invisible nylon thread
Top tension	Normal
Bobbin thread	Polyester to match fabric
Bobbin tension	Normal
Feed dogs	Raised
Stitch pattern	Straight
Stitch length	2.5 - 3
Stitch width	0

Sew on several of the straight lines or very simple curved lines in the pattern.

Transferring the Design with Free-Motion Embroidery

For more complex curves, change to the free-motion embroidery setting.

Machine foot	Free-motion
Top thread	Polyester to match fabric or invisible nylon thread
Top tension	Normal
Bobbin thread	Polyester to match fabric
Bobbin tension	Normal
Feed dogs	Lowered or covered
Stitch pattern	Straight
Stitch length	0
Stitch width	0

Stitch around the curved lines of your chosen pattern. Run the machine at a medium to fast speed and move your hands steadily without jerking the work. The pattern to be embroidered with a contrast thread will now be visible on the back of the work.

Once the design is outlined you will be able to turn the work over and see the outlines clearly on the back. You are now ready to begin embroidering with a thicker decorative thread in the bobbin from the wrong side.

Embroidering the Design Using a Decorative Thread in the Bobbin

Machine foot	Free-motion
Top thread	Polyester to match fabric
Top tension	Normal to slightly tightened
Bobbin thread	Decorative contrast thread
Bobbin tension	Loosened several degrees
Feed dogs	Lowered or covered
Stitch pattern	Straight
Stitch length	0
Stitch width	0
Fabric	Wrong side up

Outlining or Filling in the Shapes

Turn the work so that the wrong side is on top. Bring the thick bobbin thread up through the fabric by turning the hand wheel towards you. Hold the thread ends gently as you begin to sew. Outline an area by sewing over the design lines. Fill in an area by stitching small overlapping circles. Run the machine at a steady medium to fast speed. Finish by leaving a 6" tail of the thicker bobbin thread and pull this through to the wrong side of the work. Darn thread ends in by hand on the wrong side of the fabric.

Cable Stitch with Zigzag or Pattern Stitch

Machine foot	Zigzag or satin stitch
Top thread	Polyester to match fabric
Top tension	Normal
Bobbin thread	Decorative thicker thread
Bobbin tension	Loosened several degrees
Feed dogs	Raised
Stitch pattern	Straight or automatic pattern
Stitch length	0.6-3 (may need to be lengthened – see below)
Stitch width	0-5
Fabric	Wrong side up

Some pattern stitches can be very effective when used with a decorative bobbin thread. However, you may need to make some adjustments to the stitch setting to compensate for the extra thickness of the thread. Some satin stitch and decorative patterns may need to have the stitch lengthened, to avoid the thick thread bunching up too closely. Make several sample swatches to determine which stitch patterns will best suit your requirements.

Quilting

All the projects in this book are made with one or more layers of quilt batting. There are various types of batting to choose from, depending on what you are making.

For the smaller projects I have used one or more layers of light-weight fusible quilt batting to stabilize the embroidery and to add a raised, sculptured appearance. The Christmas Tree Skirt on page 75, and the Vest and the Jacket on pages 64 and 70 are examples of this method. The fusible batting can be attached to the back of the fabric and will remain firmly in place during embroidery. Read more about this on page 22.

Larger projects, such as some of the quilts, have a layer of light-or medium-weight fusible batting behind the embroidery and an additional full layer of Hobbs Heirloom™ cotton quilt batting with scrim applied. The quilt backing is applied in the usual way and then machine quilted. The machine quilting usually follows the design lines or seams in the quilt top. As the embroidery and beading are the featured surface texture rather than the quilting, the quilting lines follow the main design or seam lines in the quilt top and are inconspicuous. Some areas are stipple quilted with a meandering line of free-motion machine embroidery to add a textural contrast. For additional stability, the quilting is done with a matching polyester thread in the needle and the bobbin.

For those of you who prefer to quilt your project by hand or machine in a more elaborate design, go right ahead. Enjoy!

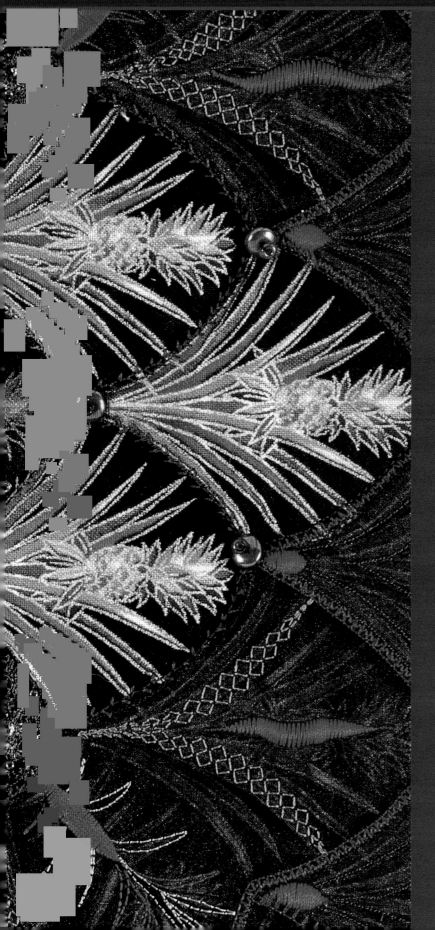

Pattern Matching

*A*ccurate pattern matching begins with accurate cutting. Mark your template with some of the design lines from the fabric, so you can line up the edges exactly before you cut. Take care when handling the cut pieces, so the edges don't stretch. Pin the seams carefully placing pins at right angles to the cut edge so that the point of the pin goes exactly through the mirror image part of the fabric design on each piece. Check the placement of the design as you sew to each pin, removing it carefully. Press the seams carefully, using an up and down pressing movement of the iron rather than sliding it, which can cause distortion.

Sample of folded edge joined with fusing

Another method for matching patterns is to fuse a folded edge. The patterns at the join can be matched exactly and stay matched without distortion while you sew along a bias edge. Use a seam guide to carefully press under the 1/4" seam allowance on one piece, then add a 1/8" strip of fusible web along the folded edge. Place the folded edge in position over the other fabric piece, with a 1/4" seam allowance. Nudge the folded edge into position so patterns match precisely, then press the seam using an up and down movement of the iron. The fabric pieces will be fused together at the seam. Fold over the top piece so the two pieces are right sides together and stitch on the seam line.

Using Mirrors

If the border you selected has a vertical or vertical and horizontal axis of symmetry, you will be able to join shapes to make mirror images. This was done in the Paisley Quilt, page 86, the Picture Frame, page 48, the Vest, page 64, and the Christmas Tree skirt, page 75. You need a clear plastic template for angles other than 45°, for example, those made in the Christmas Tree Skirt.

Using Templates

Since matching patterns is a precise art and templates can be slippery, spray the back of the template lightly with fabric adhesive. You can reposition the template as needed to select your pattern. When you are ready to cut, press the template securely into place and cut around it.

Triangle ruler with mirror showing how the mitered corner will look if cut and joined at that point.

Place the triangle ruler or template in position on the fabric. Hold the mirror so the edge rests on the fabric or the ruler at the point where the fabric will be sewn. Gently remove the template and the fabric pattern will be reflected, showing the pattern you will get when shapes like this are cut and joined. If you use two mirrors taped together to make a hinge, you will be able to open these like a book, and place them around the top point of the template and see how the complete repeat of your design will look. When you are satisfied with the positioning of the pattern, replace the template, remove the mirrors and mark the fabric. Remember to add seam allowances before cutting out the pieces.

CHAPTER 4

Beading

*B*eading adds the final touch of richness and sparkle to your project. Beads can be glass, metallic, pottery, stone, or plastic in an enormous variety of colors and sizes. I find bead shops irresistible. Whenever I travel, I seek out bead shops. I think of them as wonderful sources of calorie-free, guiltless delight that I can add to my collection. In Alaska I was in heaven with more bead shops than I had ever seen before. My luggage is always full of tiny glittering packages when I return home to Australia, reminding me of some of the wonderful places I have visited. Once, a package in my hand luggage burst, and like Tinkerbell I left a sparkling trail behind me as I dashed through the airport rushing to make a tight connection.

How Many Beads do I Need for a Project?

When beginning a large project, like some of the quilts in this book, you need to be sure that you have sufficient beads to complete the project. So, before you start beading, take the time to make a sample swatch using one of the repeats of the border fabric. Either stitch or place the beads in position, and count the number used for one repeat of the border. Multiply this by the number of repeats used in the project, and you'll know in advance how many beads you'll need. Save precious beads for special accent areas, and use readily available small round (seed) beads and bugle beads for the bulk of the project.

Beads and measuring tools

If you don't have a tiny bead scale, like the ones used in the bead shops, you can speed up bead counting. Fill a thimble, bead scoop, salt spoon, or other tiny container right to the brim with one kind of beads. Tip out the container and count the beads. Then see how many times that container can be filled from the quantity of beads you have left. This will give you a reasonably close estimate of how many you have available.

If you can't match the exact color of beads to complete a large area, choose a bead of the same size and similar in color and mix the two shades before you begin beading. When the beads are attached to the project, the two colors will blend, and give a shaded effect. This can be very attractive if you are filling large areas with randomly spaced beads.

Sew your beads whichever way you prefer, by hand or machine. I stitch my beads by hand, using a double strand of polyester thread, in a matching color. A thread lubricant keeps snarls and tangles at bay. Take a tiny backstitch after every few beads, so if one bead becomes loose or dislodged, you won't lose the whole string. Take care not to pull too tightly on the beading thread, as this will distort the backing. Don't allow the beading thread to show on the quilt backing or lining, unless you choose to combine hand quilting and beading to secure some larger areas.

If you are beading a project that will receive a lot of handling, such as the Tote Bag on page 81, bead only the display side of the bag, not the side that will be carried next to the body. Be especially vigilant about securing the threads every few beads. Keep beads stitched close to the fabric rather than creating fragile, long, dangling trails, or clusters that may become entangled with clothing. If you're beading a quilt or project such as the Table Runner on page 44, which may be displayed on a table, remember that beads will make the surface uneven, so confine your decoration to the borders of the quilt, leaving the center flat to allow placement of platters, or other ornaments.

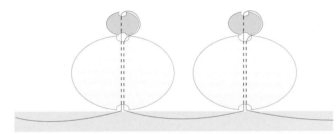

Attaching a larger bead with a smaller one on top.

I store my beads in round transparent plastic stackers. I have a small tray covered with black felt on which I place the beads with which I am working, in small, separate heaps. This makes it easy to scoop up the bead with the point of the needle, and it facilitates replacing the beads in their containers when I'm finished. A teaspoon or beader's fingernail, like a clip-on artificial fingernail is also useful for scooping up tiny beads. Keep a small container nearby, lined with a damp tissue, for trapping snipped thread ends and any discarded beads, which are damaged or unusable. In some cases when I travel, and I feel the urge to stitch beads during a quiet night in a hotel, I find that a small terry cloth hand towel makes a good substitute bead tray, as the loops stop the beads from rolling around.

The bead charts and diagrams in this book serve as suggestions only. Don't panic if you don't have the exact beads described. Look through your collection, and make an individual statement based on what you do have. Beading is an individual art, and you can make your project unique by changing the color and design of the beading and embroidery on the project. Have fun experimenting.

Note: In this book all beads are round and made of glass unless otherwise noted.

CHAPTER 5

Projects

ime for some fun!

- Heart Cushion
- Christmas Angel Table Runner
- Picture Frame
- Frog and Lizard Quilt
- Casbah Quilt
- Vest
- Jacket
- Christmas Tree Skirt
- Tote Bag
- Paisley Quilt

MATERIALS

1 1/2-yards border fabric

2/3-yard co-coordinating pink fabric for cushion

2/3-yard striped fabric for ruffle

Fabric adhesive spray

Tear-away stabilizer

Template plastic

Marking pen

18" square firm weight fusible quilt batting

16" zipper for cushion

18" square cushion insert form

Cream colored polyester thread for bobbin and
   construction

Beads

Quantities are approximate.

12	4mm blue
24	3mm blue
24	3mm mauve
24	3mm dark pink
48	3mm dark green
100	2mm light pink
140	2mm pale blue

Sulky Embroidery Thread

1177 Avocado (Pale green)

2102 Variegated rose (Pink)

2134 Variegated golden yellow

1242 Nassau blue

1119 Dark mauve

7010 Dark copper (Metallic)

METHOD

Trace and cut out the heart template pattern. Enlarge
the given pattern by approximately 550% to create
the template.

1. Make a heart template as shown. Mark the vertical
line in the center of the heart and place the template
on the border fabric to select the portion of the design
that you wish to use. Make sure the horizontal lines
in the pattern are at right angles to the vertical centerline on the heart. Trace around the heart and cut out.

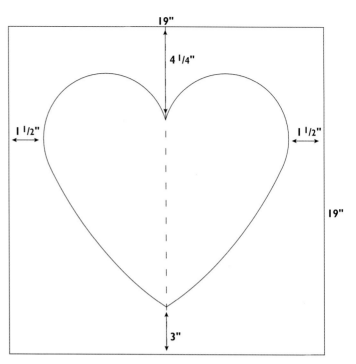

Pattern for heart template

2. Cut a 19" square of the pink background fabric
and mark a vertical line down the center.

3. Cut one 18" square of fusible quilt batting. Center
it on the wrong side of the pink background fabric
and fuse into place.

Template placement on fabric

4. Spray the back of the heart template with fabric adhesive and carefully center it on the right side of the pink background fabric. Smooth into position.

5. Rough-cut a generous sized piece of fusible tear-away stabilizer larger than the heart shape and fuse it to the back of the batting.

6. Sew four rows of straight stitch across the heart, following the design lines, to secure it to the background. Using a zigzag or walking foot with matching rose pink thread, sew around the edge of the heart with a narrow zigzag stitch. The final embroidery will cover these first rows of stitching.

Copper embroidery

Embroidery

Embroider the areas shown in bright yellow using copper metallic thread. Use a satin stitch setting—width 2—for the fence posts.

Use a free-motion setting and straight stitch to scribble over the hair.

Attaching heart to background with a zigzag stitch.

Pale green embroidery

Using a pale green thread, sew the areas shown in bright red.

Use a narrow satin stitch around the bushes and along the vine. Use a small individual satin stitch pattern unit or tapered satin stitches on the leaves.

████ Variegated pink embroidery

Using a variegated pink thread, stitch the areas shown bright red. Using a free-motion embroidery setting with straight stitch, make small round scribbles on each of the roses at the top of the heart shape.

Using a free-motion setting and straight stitch, scribble small circular lines of pink over the dress.

Using a narrow satin stitch setting—width 2—sew lines of satin stitch down the darker pink stripes at the bottom of the heart shape.

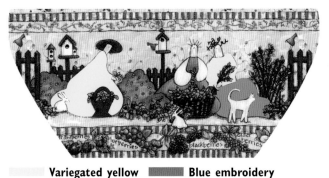

████ Variegated yellow   ████ Blue embroidery

Using a free-motion setting and straight stitch, scribble small circular lines on the yellow dresses.
Using a straight stitch follow the pattern of lines on the blue dress.

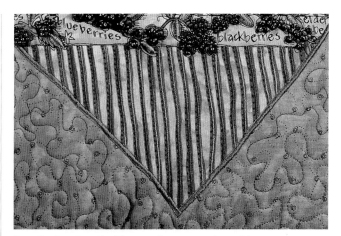

Detail of satin stitching on bottom point of heart

Assembly

When all the embroidery is complete, using a dark mauve thread and satin stitch setting—width 3—sew all around the edge of the heart shape, covering the raw edges and the first zigzag stitches.

End with a few tiny straight stitches to secure the threads. Clip and trim all thread ends.

Remove the tear-away stabilizer from the back of the embroidery, tear away the stabilizer from the batting.

Pink stipple quilting on background

Using a free-motion setting and straight stitch, stipple quilt the background in a meandering movement.

Beading

Bead the cushion front, following the illustration.

BEAD CHART FOR HEART CUSHION	
●	4mm blue
●	3mm blue
●	3mm mauve
▲	3mm dark pink
●	3mm dark green
●	2mm light pink
●	2mm pale blue

Detail of beading

Ruffle

Fold along the lengthwise grain and press the remaining beige rose sprig fabric that you cut from the border section.

1. Cut four 8"-wide strips across the remaining width of the pressed and folded sprig fabric (cut from the border). Join the ends to make a long strip.

2. Cut four 5 1/2"-wide strips across the width of the pink striped fabric. Join the ends.

3. Fold each strip in half lengthwise and press.

4. Place the raw edges of the units together to form a double layer and baste with a double row of gathering stitches.

5. Divide the ruffle into quarters, then eighths. Mark to insure even placement around the cushion. Mark the center point of each side of the cushion top.

6. Pull up the gathers evenly to fit the cushion edge, matching the markings on the ruffle to the center points and the corners.

7. Pin the ruffle to the right side of the cushion top and sew with a 5/8" seam.

Assembly

1. Cut two 18 1/4" x 10" pieces of pink fabric for the back of the cushion cover.

2. Insert the zipper using your favorite method. Open the zipper and with right sides together, sew the cushion back to the cushion front.

3. Trim the corners and seams and turn the cushion cover right side out. Press the seams and place the cushion form inside the cover.

Christmas Angel Table Runner

42" x 28"

This festive table runner can also double as a wall quilt during the holiday season. All the naive country angels in this striped border face towards the left, so the border can be cut with mitered corners, with the angels continuing around the edge of the quilt. If you wish to change the dimensions of the quilt, calculate the finished size based on the number of angel pattern repeats you wish to use, rather than try to fit the pattern repeat into pre-determined dimensions. Cut one long and one short end of the rectangular frame, and then use these pieces as templates for the other two pieces so the pattern will match exactly.

MATERIALS

1 1/3-yards border fabric

1/2-yard red fabric

1 1/3-yards fabric for backing

1/3-yard for binding

43" x 29" firm weight fusible quilt batting or regular quilt batting

Green, red, and brown polyester threads for quilting

Template plastic

Beads

Quantities are approximate.

66	6mm green bugle
50	6mm gold bugle
66	6mm red bugle
66	3mm red
550	3mm orange
121	3mm green
66	2mm bronze
165	2mm orange
165	2mm red matte

Sulky Embroidery Thread

1147 Christmas red

1051 Christmas green

1168 True orange

7010 Dark copper

Make a pattern for templates to suit the need of your own pattern repeat.

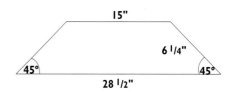

Patterns for border

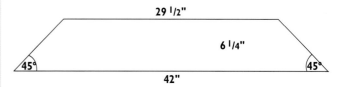

METHOD

1. Make the templates as shown.

2. Cut a 15" x 29 1/2" rectangle for the center panel.

3. Spray the templates with fabric adhesive and place them on the border fabric. Smooth them into place.

4. Cut two short units and two long units.

5. Join the sections to the central red panel and miter the corners using your favorite method. Press seams.

Template placement on fabric

6. Fuse a layer of heavy fusible quilt batting to the back of the table runner top.

Central panel with stipple quilting and feather stitch seam

Embroidery

Using a brown polyester thread and a free motion setting with straight stitch, sew a meandering stipple quilt pattern over the entire red central panel.

Using green thread and an automatic pattern stitch, sew a feather stitch pattern in the ditch of the seam between the red central panel and the border.

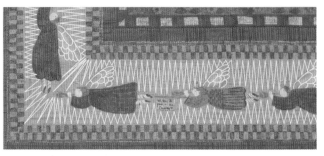

Copper embroidery

Using a free-motion setting and straight stitch, sew close lines of stitching in the beige background area behind the angels, radiating the lines at the corners.

Sew small feather-shaped loops on the angel wings.

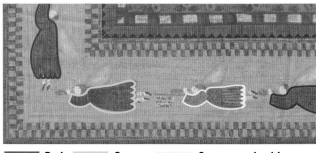

Red   Green   Orange embroidery

Using a small triangular pattern stitch, sew around the outside of the red line on the fabric.
Using a narrow satin stitch width—1.5—sew around the edge of the red angels.

Use the same satin stitch to sew around the edges of the orange and green angels with thread of matching colors.

Quilting and binding

Add the quilt backing and binding. Quilt along the main straight lines of the outside border.

Beading

Bead the quilt following the bead chart shown. Secure the thread with backstitches every so often, so if one bead becomes detached the whole lot doesn't unravel.

BEAD CHART FOR CHRISTMAS ANGEL TABLE RUNNER

▬	6mm red bugle
▭	6mm green bugle
▯	6mm gold bugle
●	3mm orange
△	3mm bronze
●	3mm green
●	3mm red
▲	2mm red
△	2mm orange

Detail of beading

17" x 17" frame

A formal border richly embroidered and beaded in shimmering metallic colors creates an elegant frame for a photo, mirror, or special artwork. By adding or subtracting pattern repeats for the size you desire, you can easily make the frame larger or smaller or change its shape to a rectangle.

MATERIALS

1-yard border fabric

1/2-yard fusible quilt batting or regular quilt batting

2 1/2-yards of 1/4" tubular flexible braid, gold

Tracing paper or plastic for template

Heavy cardboard for frame

Craft fabric glue

17" square black felt

Black polyester thread for bobbin

Heavier weight bobbin thread, copper/black for cable
  stitching

Beads

Quantities are approximate.

13	7mm gold bugle
104	6mm faceted gold oval
24	5mm flat gold disc
72	5mm flat copper disc
324	4mm bronze round
380	3mm copper round
80	2mm bronze
7	2mm gold

Sulky Metallic Thread

7010 Dark copper

7004 Dark gold

METHOD

1. Measure and cut the cardboard to the exact size of the required frame.

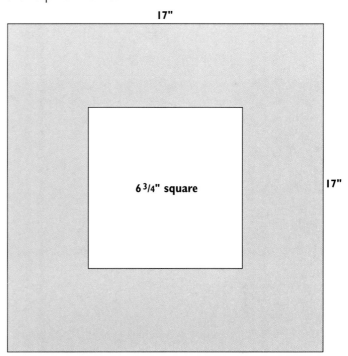

Frame dimensions

2. Make a template, as shown, in paper or plastic. Use one side of the cardboard frame to size the template. Mark the vertical line at the center of the template. Spray the back with fabric adhesive.

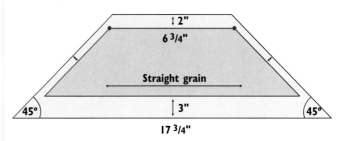

Pattern for template with seam allowances included

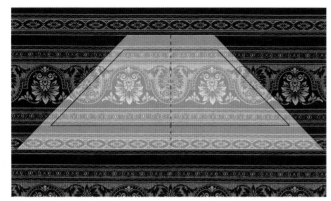

Template on fabric

3. Place the centerline of the template exactly on the center of one of the fabric motifs, with the straight grain arrow parallel to the selvage. Smooth into place.

4. Add 1/4" seam allowance and 2" extra folding fabric on the top, and 3" on the bottom.

5. Cut four identical pieces of fabric, as shown.

6. Pin and sew the seams matching patterns exactly. Press.

Joining the shapes

7. Transfer the red dots shown on the pattern onto the fabric intersections since the stitches will be picked back to these points when the frame is mounted on the cardboard.

Joining the seams

8. Using the cardboard frame as a template, cut a piece of firm fusible quilt batting. Fuse it to the wrong side of the fabric frame.

9. Cut one 17" square of black felt.

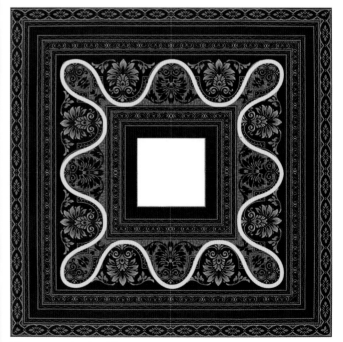

Placement for braid

Detail of stitching on braid

Embroidery

Use an open toe or satin stitch foot with gold metallic thread. Sew the tubular braid over the design lines on the fabric using a zigzag or serpentine stitch.

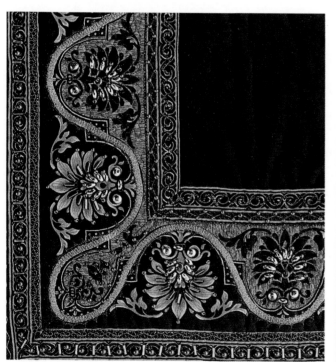

Detail of embroidery

Gold and copper embroidery

Add your selection of embroidery stitches, following the lines in the printed fabric as a guide.

If you wish to use a heavier contrast thread in the bobbin, first make a line of straight stitching using regular polyester thread and following the pattern on the right side of the fabric. This will be used as a guideline for the contrast thread that is sewn with the wrong side of the fabric on top.

Wind the thicker thread onto the bobbin, and loosen the bobbin tension slightly.

Use a black polyester thread for the needle, at normal tension. Always make a test sample on scrap fabric first to fine tune any adjustments.

Leave 6" tails of the thicker bobbin thread at the beginning and end of the stitching, and use a hand needle to pull them through to the wrong side and secure the threads.

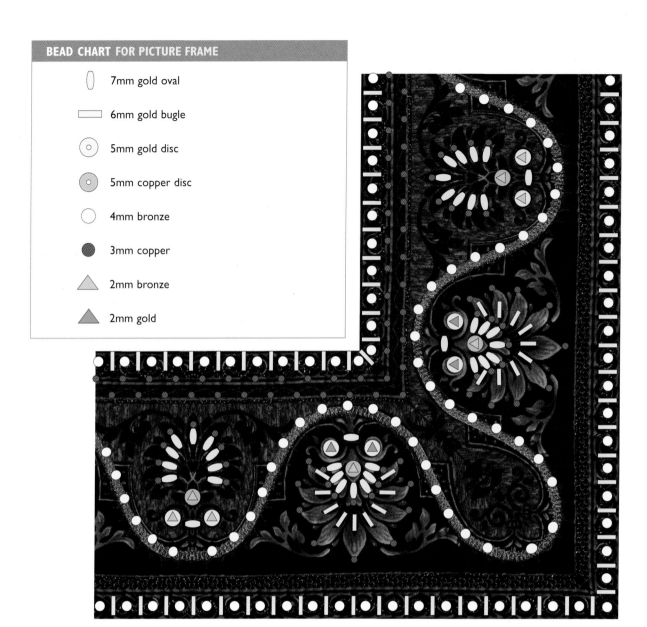

BEAD CHART FOR PICTURE FRAME

⬭	7mm gold oval
▭	6mm gold bugle
⊙	5mm gold disc
◉	5mm copper disc
◯	4mm bronze
●	3mm copper
△	2mm bronze
▲	2mm gold

Beading

Before you start, check that you have sufficient beads to finish the project. Bead the frame, using a double strand of black polyester thread. Secure threads with a tiny back stitch after every three or four beads.

Assembly

1. Place the embroidered fabric wrong-side up on the table and position the cardboard frame on top of it.

2. Pick out the stitches to the red dots at all four inner corners.

3. Turn the fabric over the frame edge to the wrong side of the cardboard. Miter the corners on the back and fasten with masking tape. When you are satisfied with the placement and the fabric is evenly stretched, glue or sew securely in place.

4. Place the photograph behind the frame and tape it into position.

5. Add the square of black felt over the back of the frame and glue or sew in position.

6. Attach a hanging loop of cord across the back of the frame. Or rest the frame on a small decorative brass stand.

45" square

The method of creating a quilt using border fabric is suitable for borders with no axis of symmetry, such as this colorful stripe fabric. The size of the center medallion is governed by the number of repeats of the pattern you wish to use in the surrounding border. You can get an approximate size to begin with, and then count the number of whole repeated units that will come closest to your requirements. As the motifs in this example—the frogs and lizards—are not arranged symmetrically, you can use an inset triangle at the end of the border strips, or even just butt the border joins together. The finished size of the quilt is 45" square.

MATERIALS

2-yards border fabric
1 1/2-yards backing fabric
1 1/2-yards purple star fabric
1 1/2-yards navy fabric
Fusible quilt batting or regular quilt batting
Tear-away fusible stabilizer
Fine black crochet cotton
Polyester threads for bobbin, quilting and beading, in navy, purple, green

Beads

Quantities are approximate.

172	6mm green iris bugle
216	3mm purple
561	3mm red
400	2mm turquoise
400	2mm dark blue
360	2mm yellow
300	2mm orange
264	2mm green metallic
232	2mm red matte
175	2mm lilac
172	2mm green glass
152	2mm gold

Sulky Embroidery Thread

1177 Avocado (Lime green)
1302 Eggplant
1246 Orange flame
1024 Goldenrod (Yellow)
1039 True red
1513 Wild peacock (Turquoise)

METHOD

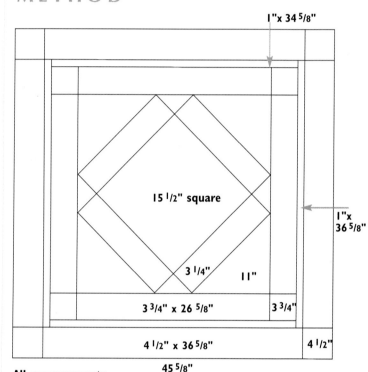

All measurements are finished sizes.

1. Cut four lizard border strips 5 3/4" x 20". Trim excess later. Cut stabilizer to match and fuse to the backs of the lizard strips.

2. Cut four frog border strips 6 1/4" x 31 1/8". Trim excess later. Cut stabilizer to match and fuse it to the backs of the frog strips.

Embroidery

Frog and lizard fabric detail

▨ Lime green embroidery on lizard fabric
▨ Red embroidery on lizard fabric
▨ Yellow embroidery on lizard fabric
▨ Orange embroidery on lizard fabric
▨ Turquoise embroidery on lizard fabric

▨ Lime green embroidery on frog fabric
▨ Eggplant embroidery on frog fabric

Embroider the Lizard strips using matching color threads and beginning with a line of suitable scallop pattern along the back of each lizard. Using a lime green thread, sew a line of tapered satin stitches down the center of each of the larger leaves.

1. Remove the stabilizer. Press and trim the lizard strips to 3 3/4" x 16".

2. Embroider the frog strips. Sew veins on the leaves in lime green, using a narrow satin stitch—width 1.5. Begin and end with tiny stitches.

3. Outline the leaves in eggplant thread using a narrow zigzag stitch—width 1.5—stitched over fine black crochet cotton. Trim the excess crochet cotton.

4. Remove the stabilizer. Press and trim the frog strips to 4 1/4" x 27 1/8".

Detail of the center medallion

Assembly

1. Cut one 16" square of purple star fabric for the center.

2. Cut one 5 7/8" square of the same fabric. Cut it diagonally twice to make quarter square-triangles. Sew them to the ends of two of the strips.

3. Sew the two lizard strips to opposite sides of the square. Then sew the strips with the attached triangles to the remaining two sides.

4. Cut two 11 7/8" squares of blue fabric. Cut them diagonally once to make half-square triangles. Sew them to lizard borders.

5. Cut four 4 1/4" squares and sew them to the ends of two frog strips.

6. Sew two frog strips to opposite sides of the center portion of the quilt. Sew the remaining frog strips to the top and bottom.

7. Cut two 1 1/2" x 34 5/8" strips of the rainforest fabric and add them to the top and bottom of the quilt.

8. Cut two 1 1/2" x 36 5/8" strips of the same fabric and add them to the sides.

9. Cut four 5" x 36 5/8" strips and four 5" squares of the star fabric and add the squares to the ends of two strips.

10. Sew two strips to the sides of the quilt. Sew the remaining strips with squares to the top and bottom.

FINISHING

Assemble the quilt, adding the batting and the backing. The quilt is quilted in straight lines along the main seam lines. The central purple panel is quilted in a diagonal 1" grid. The blue triangles at the corners are stipple quilted. The outside border of purple fabric is quilted in parallel rows one inch apart. Add the binding and finish the quilt.

Beading

Bead the lizards following the pattern of spots or stripes on the bodies. The frogs are scattered with beads that match their bodies.

Lizard beading detail

BEAD CHART FOR FROG AND LIZARD QUILT

▭ 6mm green iris bugle		◼ 2mm green metallic	
● 3mm red		△ 2mm gold	
● 3mm purple		▲ 2mm red	
● 2mm lilac		▲ 2mm dark blue	
● 2mm turquoise		▲ 2mm green	
○ 2mm yellow		▲ 2mm orange	

23 ¹/₂" x 32 ¹/₂"

The beautiful blues and exotic decorations seen in Eastern mosques inspired this quilt. I had many lovely samples of fabrics and borders in shades of blue, and thought it would be fun to combine these, using simple butt joins at the corner, as there was not enough of any one fabric to create a full border with mitered corners. This is a good project for using up precious scraps in your stash! The beaded pendant in the center is reminiscent of an antique oil lamp.

MATERIALS

Selection of border fabrics in different shades of blue, maximum length one yard

1/2-yard green fabric for central panel of quilt

1-yard blue floral fabric for backing, sashing and binding

1/2-yard blue for outer border

1/3-yard blue/purple paisley fabric

Firm weight fusible quilt batting or regular quilt batting

Polyester thread in blues and navy for bobbin and quilting

Beads for Casbah Quilt

Quantities are approximate.

146	8mm textured pearl oval
336	7mm dark blue bugle
42	5mm pearl oval
44	4mm dark blue
124	3mm turquoise
43	3mm gold metallic
474	2mm dark blue
610	2mm lilac

Beads for Pendant

8	8mm textured pearl oval
42	7mm green iris bugle
24	7mm dark blue bugle
1	5mm blue iridescent
15	4mm purple iridescent
52	3mm dark blue
11	3mm gold metallic
77	2mm turquoise

Sulky Embroidery Thread

1194 Light purple

1252 Bright peacock

7004 Dark gold

METHOD

1. Cut and fold a 10" x 16 1/4" piece of tracing paper in half. Draw the archway shape and cut it out. Place this template on the paisley fabric. Center the design on the print. Cut the fabric.

2. Cut one 16 1/4" x 18 1/4" rectangle of the green fabric.

3. Cut two 2" x 14" strips of the blue border fabric for the columns.

4. Spray the archway shape with fabric adhesive and place it into position at the top of the green rectangle, matching the raw edges, and aligning the patterns.

5. Fold and press a 1/4" seam on each side of the column strips, spray with adhesive and place in position as shown, tucking the ends under the archway.

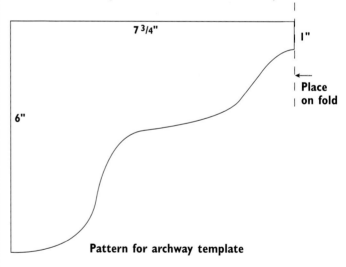

Pattern for archway template

Assembly

1. Using matching thread, sew a straight stitch down each side of the columns, close to the fold and around the edge of the archway to hold the appliqué in position.

2. Cut two 4 1/2 x 16" strips of the blue paisley border fabric, centering the design. Sew them to the top and bottom of the panel.

3. Cut two 1 1/2" x 16" strips of blue floral fabric. Sew them to the top and bottom of the quilt. Cut two 1 1/2" x 27 3/4" strips. Sew them to the sides.

4. Cut two 3" x 18" strips of blue fabric, centering the design. Sew them to the top and bottom of the quilt. Cut two 3" x 32 3/4" strips. Sew them to the sides. Measure the top.

5. Cut one piece of firm weight fusible quilt batting to the size of the quilt, and fuse it to the back of the quilt top.

░░░░░ Turquoise embroidery
▓▓▓▓▓ Light purple embroidery

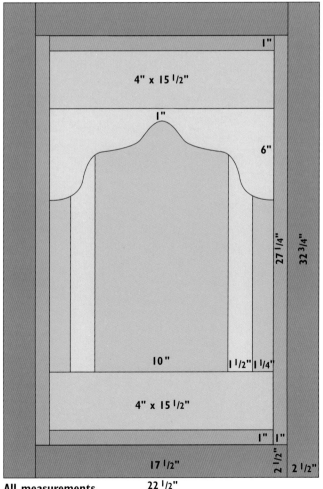

All measurements are finished size.

Embroidery

Embroider the quilt top.

Select a satin stitch setting, and using a turquoise thread sew a line of satin stitch—width 4—along the curved edge of the archway.

Select a suitable spiked pattern stitch and sew along the straight black line in the paisley pattern at the top and bottom of the quilt.

Select a small star pattern to sew around the semi-circles in the paisley pattern strips.

Using a light purple thread and a free-motion setting, scribble the bottom of the blue paisley strip only at the top of the quilt.

Select an automatic pattern stitch with small triangles, and sew along the seam between the paisley strip and the top of the archway. Sew a narrow line of satin stitch—width 1"—down the inside edges of the columns.

Gold embroidery

Stipple the entire archway shape using a gold thread in the needle and a dark blue thread in the bobbin.

Select an automatic stitch with a star pattern and sew a line of stars 1/4" inside the turquoise edge of the archway.

Sew a line of the same star stitch pattern in the seam at the bottom of the paisley border fabric at the bottom of the quilt.

Sew a line of spiked scallop pattern stitch over the turquoise satin stitch, and sew a line of the same pattern down the outside edges of the columns.

Sew rows of satin stitch—width 3—along the center of the paisley border at the top and the bottom, following the curved lines in the printed fabric.

Quilting

Add the quilt backing and stipple quilt the center green areas, using a matching green polyester thread. Use a matching blue polyester thread to quilt in the ditch of all the straight seams.

Stitch in the ditch of all straight seams using a matching blue polyester thread. Bind the quilt with the blue floral fabric.

Beading

BEAD CHART FOR ARCHWAY AND COLUMN	
⬭	8mm textured pearl oval
▮	7mm dark blue bugle
●	4mm dark blue
▪	3mm dark blue
△	2mm lilac

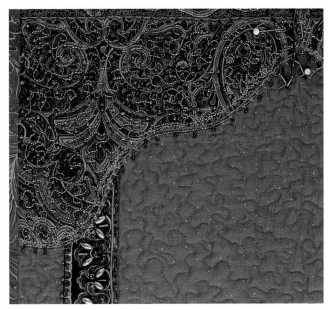

Detail of column beading

Detail of border beading

BEAD CHART FOR BORDERS

8mm textured pearl oval

7mm dark blue bugle

5mm pearl oval

3mm gold metallic

2mm dark blue

2mm lilac

3mm turquoise

PENDANT

Cut a 2" square of the archway fabric, press a $^1/4$" seam allowance on each side. Fold under two opposite corners $^3/8$". Then fold the square in half to make a shape as shown. Hand sew the edges together.

Beading

Bead the pendant. Make a hanging cord with bugle beads and small round turquoise beads. Hand sew the pendant in place at the center of the archway.

BEAD CHART FOR PENDANT	
	8mm textured pearl oval
	7mm green iris bugle
	7mm dark blue bugle
	5mm blue iridescent
	4mm purple iridescent
	3mm gold metallic
	3mm dark blue
	2mm turquoise

Actual size

Pendant

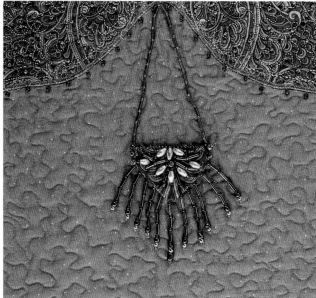

Detail of beaded pendant

Vest

A vest is a wonderful fashion accessory and a great way to show off your embroidery skills. Here a matte jacquard fabric combines beautifully with a paisley border enriched with a sheer overlay and sparkling beads.

MATERIALS

Vest pattern (lined)

Cotton jacquard fabric for body of vest—use pattern yardage

1-yard paisley border fabric for appliqué

2/3-yard dark blue sheer organza fabric for overlay

Lining fabric—use pattern yardage

Light weight fusible quilt batting or regular quilt batting—use pattern yardage

Polyester thread in navy and purple

Beads

Quantities are approximate.

234   7mm faceted green iridescent oval
110   4mm blue/mauve matte bugle
24   4mm blue iris
355   2mm purple iridescent
116   2mm green iridescent
100   2mm navy iridescent
44   2mm bronze

Sulky Embroidery Thread

503   Green peacock
1194 Light purple
1195 Dark purple
1090 Deep peacock

METHOD

1. Cut out vest fronts and back in the jacquard fabric. Cut matching fusible interfacing. Trim 5/8" on seams.

2. Fuse interfacing to the wrong side of the jacquard fabric pieces making sure that all seam allowances are equal. The edge of the interfacing will be the stitching guide during assembly.

Placement of vest back on border fabric.

Back

1. Place the pattern for the vest back on a single layer of paisley fabric, as shown. Turn the pattern piece so that the border design forms a V shape that meets at the center back. The edge of the border design comes close to the outer edge of the armhole where it meets the shoulder. Add 1/4" seam allowance to the center back.

2. Trace a straight cutting line 1" outside the scalloped edge of the design. Cut out the border following this line. The excess will be trimmed later.

3. Using this piece as a template, place it face down on the face up yardage, matching patterns exactly, and cut around it to create a mirror image.

4. Sew the center back seam on the border fabric, matching pattern exactly. Press the seam open.

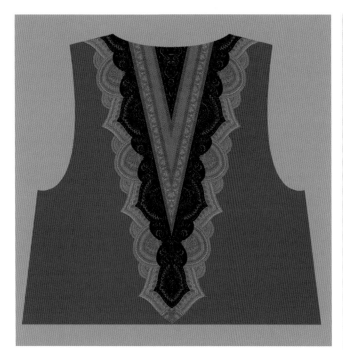

Vest back

Placement of vest front on border fabric

Front

5. Place the vest front pattern on the border fabric and select the pattern. Then follow steps 3 and 4 above to create the vest front.

6. Place the border pieces in position on the back and the fronts of the vest. Use fabric adhesive or baste in place.

7. Cover with a layer of organza. Pin or baste this in position.

8. Using a marking pen, trace the design lines for stitching and trimming on the front and back pieces.

Appliqué

Sew around the edges of the design, using a narrow zigzag stitch following the traced lines. The decorative stitching will later cover this stitching. Zigzag along neck and shoulder edges.

Detail of overlay stitched and trimmed

Use small sharp scissors to trim away excess appliqué and sheer organza close to the stitching.

Embroidery

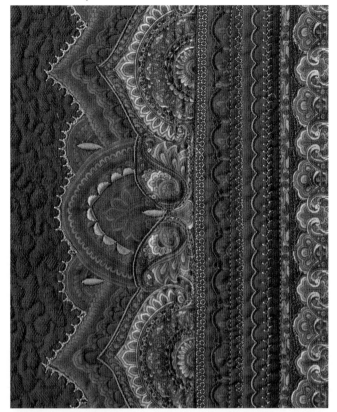

Detail of embroidery

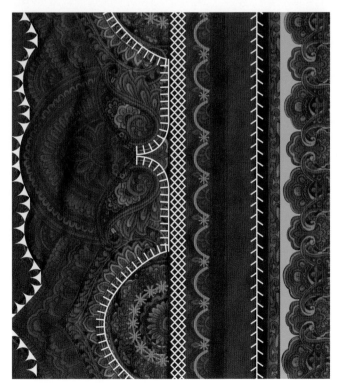

Green peacock embroidery
Dark purple embroidery
Navy blue embroidery

Select a suitable decorative pattern stitch to sew along the outer edges of the appliqué, covering the raw edges of the fabric. Sew lines of honeycomb stitch down the V shape at the center back.

Sew a line of featherstitch at the upper edges of the center back V shape.

Using a free-motion setting, straight stitch, and navy blue thread, fill in the flower shapes in the top of the center back V shape. Select a satin stitch setting and automatic patterns of small star shapes and curved lines down the V shape at the center back and around the semi-circular paisley shapes.

Deep peacock embroidery
Light purple embroidery

Select a satin stitch setting and sew narrow lines of deep peacock satin stitch—width 1—over the inside trimmed edges of the sheer organza. Sew lines of small scallops around the center back V shape. Select an automatic pattern stitch to sew semi-circles of light purple. Outline petal shapes above the semi-circles just sewn. Add more stitching according to your preference.

Assembly

Sew the vest pieces together using your favorite construction method.

Stipple quilting on body of vest

Beaded back of vest

Quilting and finishing

Using a free-motion machine setting and purple polyester thread, stipple quilt the body of the vest front and back. When the embroidery and quilting are completed, press the vest front and back from the wrong side. Cut out the vest front and back in lining fabric and complete the vest following pattern instructions.

Beading

Bead the vest front and back following the beading chart on the next page.

Detail of beading

BEAD CHART FOR VEST

	7mm faceted green iridescent oval
	4mm blue/mauve bugle
	4mm blue iris
	2mm bronze
	2mm purple iridescent
	2mm navy iridescent
	2mm green iridescent

Border fabrics can be used in fashion garments too. Add an embroidered and beaded border to your favorite jacket pattern. Clever fabric manipulation allows the straight border to flow around the curved edges of the garment. The sheer organza overlay color allows you to match the border fabric exactly to your garment fabric.

MATERIALS

Jacket pattern (lined)
Dark blue cotton for jacket—use pattern yardage
Lining fabric—use pattern yardage
Fusible lightweight quilt batting or regular batting—
    use pattern yardage for lining
1-yard border fabric, purple/green
1/2-yard navy blue organza
Polyester thread in navy

Beads

Quantities are approximate.

17	9mm purple iridescent disc
14	3mm dark blue disc
102	3mm copper
2085	2mm bronze

Sulky Embroidery Thread

7004 Dark gold
7010 Dark copper
1005 Black

METHOD

1. Cut out all jacket pattern pieces in blue cotton fabric. Cut out matching pieces of fusible quilt batting for the front, back, and sleeves. From the batting, trim all 5/8" seam allowances and trim the hem allowance from the bottom of the body and sleeves. Fuse the batting to the wrong side of the jacket pieces.

Detail of quilting on jacket

Front

1. Cut three approximately 3 1/4"-wide strips from the main border. If your pattern has a straight front, the center front borders can be directly applied to the jacket fabric. If the jacket has a curved edge front, as shown, the border will need to be curved slightly to fit around the edge.

2. Mark the 5/8" seam allowances on the center fronts and the back neck to assist with the placement of the border pieces. Place the border strip on the jacket front with the outer edge just inside the marked seam line.

3. Run several parallel rows of basting threads along the border to pull up the fullness slightly, and ease the border around the curve. Press the strip when the ease is evenly distributed.

4. Pin the border strip into position, with the edge just inside the 5/8" seam line so it will be caught when the seam is stitched. Any slight ripples in the border will be covered by the sheer organza and will not show.

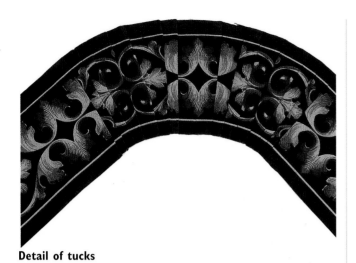

Detail of tucks

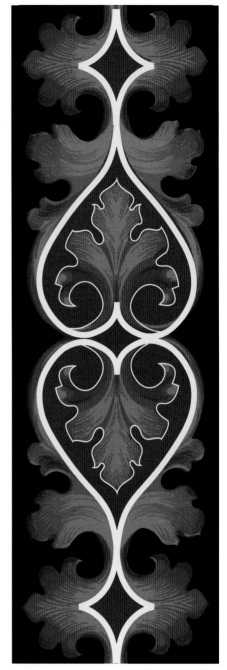

Back

1. Cut a strip of border fabric approximately twice the length of the back neckline, which has a sharper curve.

2. Center the border at the neck back. Make a series of tiny V shaped darts in the fabric until the curves match.

3. Trim the border and pin it with the edge just inside the seam line as before.

4. Cut straight strips of organza wide enough to cover the border. Sew the organza to the border strip following the lines in the fabric. Do not trim the organza or border fabric until after the embroidery is completed.

5. Using a fine marking pen, mark the lines you want to embroider on the border.

6. Using a free-motion setting and black thread, fill in the background areas of the border with a small zigzag stitch.

■ Black embroidery
▨ Gold embroidery

Embroidery

Using the free-motion setting and gold thread, outline the leaves with a straight stitch.

Changing to a satin stitch setting—width 3—outline the hearts in gold thread.

Assembly

1. When the embroidery is complete, fold back the organza and trim the excess border fabric close to the lines of straight stitching. Leave the raw edges of the organza on the front and neck edges since they will be stitched into the seam line. On the other edge, trim the organza close to the straight stitching line.

2. Cover the raw edge of the border and organza with a satin stitch—width 5, length 0.5—using navy thread.

3. Cut out the lining and complete the jacket following the pattern instructions. Leave the lower edge of the lining free until the beading is complete, and then slip stitch the lining into place.

Gold embroidery

Beading

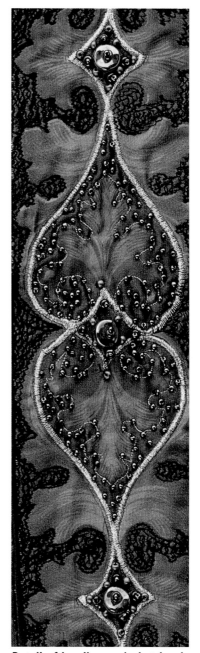

Detail of beading on jacket border

BEAD CHART FOR JACKET BORDER

9mm purple iridescent disc

3 mm dark blue disc

3mm copper

2mm bronze

Approximately 45" in diameter

This glittering tree skirt will be the star under your tree next Christmas. The subtle shades of the border print fabric are enhanced with the sparkle of beads, satin ribbons and a brilliant red crystal organza. The tree skirt shown measures approximately 45" in diameter.

MATERIALS

2 2/3-yards border fabric
1-yard bright red sheer crystal organza
1 1/3-yards bright red cotton lining fabric
1 1/3-yards firm weight fusible quilt batting
4-yards 1/8" red satin ribbon
4-yards 3/8" green satin ribbon
Black polyester thread
Red polyester thread for quilting
5 small black hooks and eyes, or Velcro® for fastening
Template Plastic

Beads

Quantities are approximate.

72	12mm bronze bugles
12	5mm flat gold discs
24	5mm bronze squares
12	4mm gold
48	4mm green
12	2mm bronze
462	2mm red
840	2mm green
300	2mm gold

Sulky Embroidery Thread

7004 Dark gold
1147 Christmas red
1051 Christmas green

METHOD

When creating the plastic template, the angles must be accurate or the skirt will not fit together. However, the lengths can be adjusted to suit your fabric or make a larger skirt. Create one template and label the face of it T. Turn it over and label the reverse side Tr.

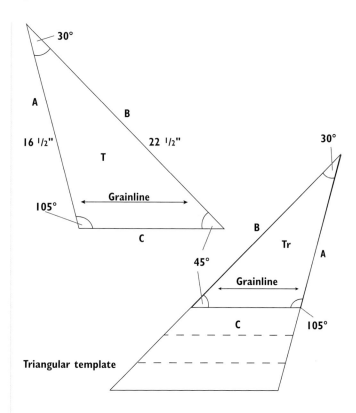

Triangular template

1. Draw line A on a piece of template plastic. Using a protractor, make a point on the line and draw line B at a 30° angle as shown. Determine the length of your skirt and draw line C across the bottom. Use the protractor to make sure all the angles are accurate.

Template T on fabric

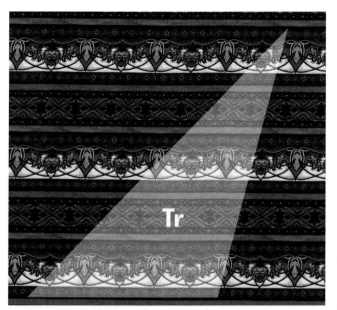

Template Tr on fabric

Triangles joined to form the tree skirt

2. Place the grainline on the lengthwise grain of your border fabric. Position a mirror against the side of the triangle to see the completed design.

3. Trace part of the fabric design and some of the stripes onto the template for precise pattern matching.

4. Cut six T triangles and six Tr triangles.

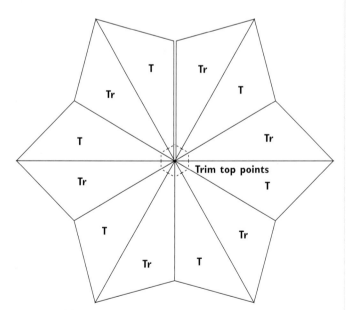

Layout of fabric triangles with top points trimmed

5. Pin the triangles together in pairs, matching the pattern. Sew with 1/4" seams to create an elongated diamond. Sew the six diamond shapes together leaving one seam open to fit around the tree. Press all seams open.

6. Cut a piece of firm weight fusible quilt batting to the same shape as the tree skirt. Trim away the 1/4" seam allowance from the batting, then fuse it into position on the back of the skirt. The batting edge will be the seam guide when attaching the lining.

7. Cut 4" x 42" strips of red organza and pin them on the outer border of the skirt. Overlap the strips 1/8" at the center of the heart shapes. These shapes will later be embroidered and the excess organza trimmed away so the joins will not show.

8. Pin 3" squares of sheer organza over the heart shapes on the inner border.

Embroidery

Using red thread, sew along the edges of the red border and around the heart shapes with a narrow zigzag stitch—width 2, length 0.5.

Red and green ribbon applied to skirt

Trim away excess organza from both edges of the outside border, and from the inside of the heart shapes. Use a free motion setting, gold thread, and straight stitch with a meandering movement, to stipple the red organza border.

Pin the green and red ribbon in position, and sew it using a feather stitch automatic pattern and matching thread. Sew both sides of the green ribbon and stitch down the center of the narrow red satin ribbon.

Red and gold embroidery

▌▌▌▌	Red embroidery
░░░░	Gold embroidery

Change to a satin stitch setting—width 2.5, length 0.5—and sew around the edges of all the heart shapes, covering the previous stitching and the raw edges. Use a very narrow zigzag—width 1.5, length 0.5—to follow the lines of the fabric pattern, then add individual petal-shaped pattern units as shown. Change to red thread. Select a suitable automatic pattern stitch, and sew over the upper and lower edges of the red organza border, covering the raw edges. Sew lines of scallops or a suitable automatic pattern following the lines in the fabric next to the red ribbon.

Select a narrow satin stitch—width 1.5, length 0.5—and follow the lines in the fabric to sew curves linking the red heart shapes.

Detail of embroidery

Select small individual petal-shaped pattern units to make flower shapes between the lines of gold embroidery. Sew one individual petal shape at each corner of the red scalloped embroidery.

Assembly

When the embroidery is complete, press the skirt gently from the wrong side.

1. Cut a piece of fabric for the backing using the tree skirt template.

2. Pin the lining to the skirt, right sides together, and stitch the outside seam only, close to the trimmed quilt batting. Trim the corners and turn the lining to the right side. Press the seam.

3. After embroidering and quilting the skirt, trim the edges of the open side.

Quilting and Finishing

Quilt the skirt by hand or machine, following the straight lines in the fabric print.

1. Trim the edges of the slit in the skirt.

2. Cut 1 1/4"–wide strips of the border fabric on the straight grain of the fabric and bind the straight edge.

3. Cut a 2"–wide bias strip of the border fabric and bind the small circle, steaming the binding to fit the curve.

4. Sew small hooks and eyes, or Velcro strips, to the straight opening to fasten the skirt.

Completed tree skirt

Beading

Bead the skirt following the bead chart on the next page.

BEAD CHART FOR CHRISTMAS TREE SKIRT

	12mm bronze bugles
	5mm gold discs
	5mm bronze squares
	4mm gold
	4mm green
	2mm bronze
	2mm gold
	2mm red
	2mm green

Tote Bag

10" x 15 ¹/₂"

In this project a border fabric has been used for the strap of a fun and glitzy tote bag. However, an all-over design fabric has been used for the body of the shoulder bag. This beautiful Indian basket fabric cried out to be encrusted with further decoration. Because the fabric design is very lively, with lots of tiny shapes and patterns, using black tulle overlay dimmed the background shapes a little. The tulle was trimmed away from the feature shapes that show up in greater contrast. The same technique could also be used for a striking vest.

MATERIALS

1/3-yard bag fabric for bag
1/2-yard striped fabric for border and strap
1/3-yard lining fabric
1/3-yard black tulle
Fusible or regular quilt batting
Black polyester thread

Beads

Quantities are approximate.

4	15mm brass buttons
2	10mm brass disks
26	8mm large hole beads, blue
20	8mm large hole beads, gold
7	8mm large hole beads, clear
8	8mm large hole beads, blue iris
3	8mm large hole beads, amber
1	5mm red
2	5mm orange
12	5mm rectangular bronze
34	5mm dark blue bugle
42	5mm gold bugle
40	5mm oval
12	4mm blue matte
14	3mm black
8	3mm red matte
6	3mm copper metallic
50	3mm white bugle
18	3mm gold bugle
145	2mm lemon
140	2mm red matte
100	2mm green

Sulky Embroidery Thread

1246 Orange flame
1242 Nassau blue
1239 Apricot (Beige)
7010 Dark Copper

METHOD

1. Cut two 10 1/2" x 12" rectangles from the bag fabric for the front and back.

2. Cut two 10" x 11 1/2" pieces of fusible quilt batting. Trim the 1/4" seam allowance on the sides. Fuse the batting to the wrong side of the fabric, leaving seam allowances equal.

3. Cut two 10 1/2" x 12" rectangles of black tulle. Pin them to the front and back of the bag.

Cover the bag fabric with the black tulle

Tulle overlay with stitching around circles

Embroidery

Sew around the outside of selected circle shapes as shown, using narrow zigzag stitch—width 2, length 0.5—and black thread in the needle and the bobbin.

Detail of embroidery on bag front

Tulle overlay with circles cut away

Trim away the tulle from inside the circles close to the stitching.

Orange embroidery

Blue embroidery

Copper embroidery

Apricot embroidery

Select suitable embroidery stitches and sew around each trimmed circle, covering the raw edges of the tulle. Use additional embroidery stitches, or individual pattern units to embellish each circle.

When all the embroidery is complete on the bag front and back, trim all thread ends. You may be inspired by the pattern printed on the fabric, which can be enhanced by additional individual pattern units or concentric circles of embroidery in contrasting colors.

Assembly

Fringe

1. Cut eighteen 1 1/2" x 12" strips from the bag and border fabrics.

2. Fold the strips in half, right sides together, and stitch 1/4" seams to form narrow tubes.

3. Turn the tubes right side out using your favorite turning method.

4. Pin the tubes to the bottom of the front of the bag; right sides together and matching raw edges. Sew them in place.

Top Borders

1. Cut two 4 1/2" x 10 1/2" strips from the striped fabric. Center the stripe design so it will fall in the center of the bag.

2. Cut a 4" x 10" strip of fusible quilt batting. Fuse it to the back of the border strip, keeping 1/4" seam allowances free to reduce bulk.

3. Sew the borders to the top of the bag front and back. Press the seam toward the bag.

4. Sew decorative pattern stitches along the seam.

Bag

1. Cut two 10 1/2" square pieces of lining.

2. Sew the lining pieces to the other side of the front and back borders. Press seams toward the borders.

3. Pin the bag front and lining to the bag back and lining, right sides together, matching seams at the borders.

4. Sew a 1/4" seam around the bag beginning at the top of the lining, sewing down the side of the bag, across the bottom, and up the other side. Leave the bottom seam of the lining open to allow for turning and ease of beading.

5. Trim the corners, turn the bag right side out and press the seams.

6. Fold the bag border in half, pushing the lining to the inside.

7. Stitch in the ditch of the seam between the bag and the border.

Strap

1. Cut a 4 1/2" x 42" strip from the border fabric. Cut a 4" x 41" piece of fusible quilt batting.

2. Place the batting on the strap. Fold the 1/4" seam allowances in on the long sides and fuse them to the batting.

3. Fold the strap in half, wrong sides together, and either slip stitch by hand or top stitch by machine. Turn in the ends.

4. Attach the strap to the inside of the bag back, butting the sides of the strap against the side seams.

Beading

The beading on the tote bag should be your own personal expression, as simple or as complex as you wish. I used a combination of seed and bugle beads, and brass buttons, echoing the patterns on the individual basket shapes. Experiment with some different color combinations, placing beads on the fabric. Refer to the detail in the photograph for some ideas. When you are satisfied with your design, sew the beads in place.

Finishing

Fold the raw edges of the lining fabric to the inside, making a narrow hem. Sew the seam. Push the lining fabric to the inside.

Thread large beads onto each fringe strip, tying a firm knot below each bead, and at the end of the fringe strips.

Detail of beaded fringe

54" square

This wall quilt glows with the richness of a magic carpet. The complex fabric print has several different borders, arranged in a mirror image. This means that one half of the fabric has the border design facing to the right, and the opposite side of the fabric has the design facing to the left. In order to create mirror image pieces that are joined to form the mitered corners, you will need to cut triangles from both sides of the fabric. Make your triangle template and trace part of the fabric design onto the triangle for precise pattern matching. The wall quilt measures 54" square.

MATERIALS

5-yards Paisley fabric
1-yard navy blue fabric for sashing and binding.
2 1/3-yards backing fabric
Lightweight fusible quilt batting
Regular quilt batting
Machine embroidery hoop
Fusible tear-away stabilizer
Template plastic

Beads

Quantities are approximate.

328	7mm gold oval
240	6mm gold bugle
496	6mm red bugle
56	4mm dark blue disc
512	3mm copper
136	3mm gold
400	3mm blue iris square
192	2mm red
104	2mm blue
320	2mm gold
88	2mm blue iris
640	2mm blue
96	2mm green iris

Sulky Embroidery Thread

1195 Dark purple
1302 Eggplant
1147 Christmas red
572 Blue ribbon
1246 Orange flame
7004 Dark gold

METHOD

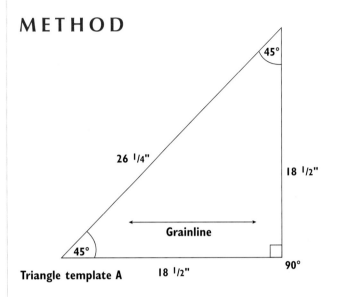

Triangle template A

45°
26 1/4"
18 1/2"
Grainline
45°
18 1/2"
90°

1. Make one 90°-triangle template, with short sides 18 1/2" long. Label the face of the triangle A, flip it over and label the other side B.

2. Trace part of the fabric design onto the template for precise matching.

3. Place the template so that one short side of the triangle is along the long edge of the border pattern and the grainline of fabric.

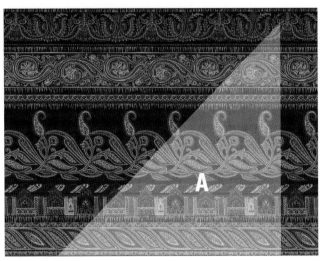

A triangle placement on fabric

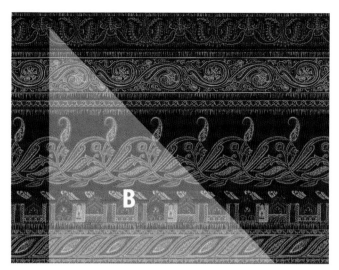

B triangle placement on fabric

4. Cut four A triangles from one edge of the paisley fabric, adding 1/4" seam allowance. Then flip the template over and cut four B triangles in the opposite direction from the opposite edge of the fabric.

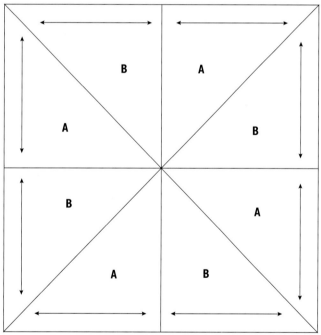

Layout of triangles

Assembly

1. Pin each A triangle to a B triangle, matching all lines and patterns precisely. Sew together to make the square center medallion. Press seams to one side.

Triangles joined to form center medallion

2. Cut one square of lightweight fusible quilt batting 1/2" smaller than the size of the center medallion square and fuse this to the back of the fabric, leaving 1/4" allowances evenly all around.

Embroidery

Use a machine embroidery hoop to stabilize the fabric. Embroider the center medallion with purple and eggplant colored threads.

For the other embroidery areas, use fusible tear-away fabric stabilizer.

Purple embroidery

Embroider the background area of the center using a free-motion setting and a narrow zigzag scribble background-filling stitch.

Eggplant embroidery

Embroider the smaller areas within the scroll shapes with eggplant colored thread, using the same free-motion setting.

Blue embroidery

Raise the feed dogs, and change the machine setting to satin stitch using an open toe satin stitch foot. Using blue thread, sew rows of pattern stitch as shown. Sew the small petal-shaped single pattern units along the inner border, and use a satin stitch tapering in width from 0 to 5 to sew the long leaf shapes in the scrolls. Choose a pattern stitch to sew units of four small triangles between the mosque shapes along the outer border.

Use red thread and satin stitch to sew long leaf shapes where indicated, tapering the stitch width from 0 to 5.

Red embroidery

Using orange thread, sew individual petal shaped units as shown, and longer lines of tapered satin stitch in the scrolls.

Select an automatic pattern stitch for around the outer border.

Orange embroidery

Gold embroidery

Use gold embroidery thread to sew a scalloped automatic pattern. Return to the satin stitch setting, stitch along the straight lines and around the outside of the scrolls.

Sew lines of narrow zigzag along the stems of the flowers. Sew long lines of tapered satin stitch at the corners of the inner square.

Select a honeycomb stitch, and fill in the columns between the mosque shapes, securing the threads at each end with a few tiny backstitches. Remove the tear-away stabilizer from the back of the embroidery.

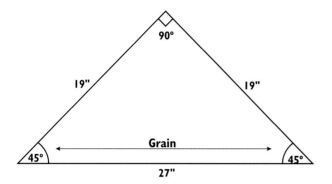

Template C for corner triangles

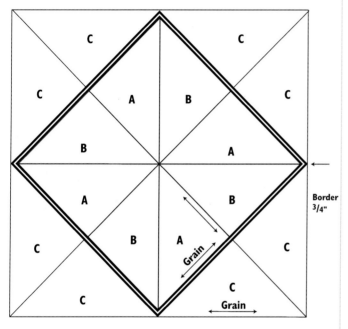

Layout for corner triangles

Assembly and finishing

1. Cut 1 1/4" sashing strips of navy blue fabric. Sew them to the outside edges of the center. Press seams.

2. Measure the sides of this square to determine the size of the corner triangles to be attached to the outsides of the center medallion.

3. Make a second 45°-triangle template C. Both short sides must be half the length of the side of the center medallion.

4. Place the longest side (hypotenuse) of the triangle on the lengthwise pattern of the border. This places the straight grain on the outer edge of the quilt, minimizing stretching.

5. Cut four triangles from one edge of the paisley fabric, and cut four triangles from the opposite edge, adding 1/4" seam allowances on each side.

6. Pin and sew the triangles together in pairs so they form mirror images. Sew the corner triangles to the center medallion.

7. Press all seams, and add the quilt batting and backing.

Quilting and binding

Quilt by hand or machine quilt following the seam lines and the main design lines on the fabric. Bind the quilt using navy blue fabric.

Beading

bead the quilt, following the bead chart on the following page.

Detail of beading on corner triangles

Outer corner triangles

BEAD CHART FOR PAISLEY QUILT

⬭ 7mm gold oval	⬤ 2mm blue
▯ 6mm gold bugle	○ 2mm gold
⬭ 6mm red bugle	○ 2mm blue iris
◉ 4mm dark blue disc	▲ 2mm blue
○ 3mm copper	△ 2mm green iris
● 2mm red	△ 3mm gold
	▪ 3mm blue iris square

Fabrics Used for the Projects

HEART CUSHION
Benartex Fabrics
Berry Patch Collection
Berry patch border 621 color 07
beige 625, color 26 light rose
Stripe 626, color 26, watermelon

CHRISTMAS ANGEL TABLE
RUNNER
Benartex Fabrics
Peace in the Country Collection
Border 570 color C Green
Frost Red QP 200 9701-C2

PICTURE FRAME
RJR Fabrics
Sumatra black/brown 3356-2

FROG AND LIZARD QUILT
Robert Kaufman Fabrics
Rainforest stripe AJS22929-1 Navy
Main Collage AJS 2290-3 Navy
Star Toss AJS 2294-6 Purple
Kona Dye Multi Print EDD 2495-1
True Navy

CASBAH QUILT
RJR Fabrics
Hidden Garden Blue 3129-1
Millenium Plume Blue 3306-2
Devonshire Purple/green: 3121-3
Border Basics, Paisley for Patchwork,
blue 2852-3
Sumatra green spot 3360-21

VEST
RJR Fabrics
Border Basics, Paisley for Patchwork
2852-4 Purple

JACKET
RJR Fabrics
Perennial Garden Border Purple
3025-1
Robert Kaufman Fabrics
Kona Dye Multi Print EDD 2495-1
True Navy

CHRISTMAS TREE SKIRT
RJR Fabrics
Border Basics 2647–3 Green

TOTE BAG
Robert Kaufman Fabrics
Native Plains collection
Indian Baskets AJS-2444-3 Blue
Navajo Stripe AJS 24445-4 Cloud

PAISLEY QUILT
Benartex Fabrics
Serendipity Collection
Paisley Border 230 Color 81 Fuchsia

RETAILERS

Beads
Bead and Button Magazine
http://www.beadandbutton.com/

Delica beads and other goodies
http://www.millhill.com

Fusible Batting
Quilters Fusible Batting™ from June
Tailor
The batting comes in three sizes—
36" x 45", 45" x 60", 90" x 108".
Check your local quilt store or
contact June Tailor 800-844-5400
for a shop nearest you.

Gold Fuse™ from Mountain Mist®
Check your local store or contact
Mountain Mist 800-543-7173 for a
shop nearest you.

Threads
The Thread Studio
6 Smith St Perth
Western Australia 6000
Phone +08 9227 1561
Fax +08 9227 0254
http://www.thethreadstudio.com
E-mail: thethreadstudioe.com
Mail-order threads, and all kinds of
associated embroidery materials,
paints, yarns etc.

Sulky of America
http://www.sulky.com/
Machine embroidery threads.

Other supplies
Cotton Patch Mail Order
3405 Hall Lane, Dept. CTB
Lafayette, CA 94549
(800) 835-4418
(925) 283-7883
E-mail: quiltusa@yahoo.com
Website: www.quiltusa.com

OTHER FINE BOOKS FROM C&T PUBLISHING

Anatomy of a Doll: The Fabric Sculptor's Handbook,
  Susanna Oroyan

*The Art of Machine Piecing: Quality Workmanship
  Through a Colorful Journey,* Sally Collins

The Art of Silk Ribbon Embroidery, Judith Baker Montano

The Art of Classic Quiltmaking, Harriet Hargrave and
  Sharyn Craig

The Artful Ribbon, Candace Kling

Baltimore Beauties and Beyond (Volume I), Elly Sienkiewicz

The Best of Baltimore Beauties, Elly Sienkiewicz

Color Play: Easy Steps to Imaginative Color in Quilts,
  Joen Wolfrom

*Cotton Candy Quilts: Using Feedsacks, Vintage and
  Reproduction Fabrics,* Mary Mashuta

Crazy Quilt Handbook, Judith Montano

Cut-Loose Quilts: Stack, Slice, Switch & Sew, Jan Mullen

Designing the Doll: From Concept to Construction,
  Susanna Oroyan

*Elegant Stitches: An Illustrated Stitch Guide & Source
  Book of Inspiration,* Judith Baker Montano

Exploring Machine Trapunto: New Dimensions, Hari Walner

*Fabric Shopping with Alex Anderson, Seven Projects to Help
  You: Make, Successful Choices, Build Your Confidence,
  Add to Your Fabric Stash,* Alex Anderson

Fancy Appliqué: 12 Lessons to Enhance Your Skills,
  Elly Sienkiewicz

Fantastic Fabric Folding: Innovative Quilting Projects,
  Rebecca Wat

Fantastic Figures: Ideas & Techniques Using the New Clays,
  Susanna Oroyan

*Finishing the Figure: Doll Costuming, Embellishments,
  Accessories,* Susanna Oroyan

Floral Stitches: An Illustrated Guide, Judith Baker Montano

Flower Pounding: Quilt Projects for All Ages, Amy Sandrin
  & Ann Frischkorn

Free Stuff for Quilters on the Internet, 2nd Ed.
  Judy Heim and Gloria Hansen

Free Stuff for Sewing Fanatics on the Internet, Judy Heim
  and Gloria Hansen

Free Stuff for Stitchers on the Internet, Judy Heim and
  Gloria Hansen

Free Stuff for Traveling Quilters on the Internet, Gloria Hansen

*Ghost Layers & Color Washes: Three Steps to Spectacular
  Quilts,* Katie Pasquini Masopust

*Hand Appliqué with Alex Anderson: Seven Projects for
  Hand Appliqué,* Alex Anderson

*Hand Quilting with Alex Anderson: Six Projects for Hand
  Quilters,* Alex Anderson

Heirloom Machine Quilting, Third Edition, Harriet Hargrave

Kaleidoscopes: Wonders of Wonder, Cozy Baker

Kaleidoscopes & Quilts, Paula Nadelstern

Mastering Machine Appliqué, Harriet Hargrave

*Mastering Quilt Marking: Marking Tools & Techniques,
  Choosing Stencils, Matching Borders & Corners,*
  Pepper Cory

*On the Surface: Thread Embellishment & Fabric
  Manipulation,* Wendy Hill

Pieced Flowers, Ruth B. McDowell

Piecing: Expanding the Basics, Ruth B. McDowell

The Quilted Garden: Design & Make Nature-Inspired Quilts,
  Jane A. Sassaman

Recollections, Judith Baker Montano

*Shadow Redwork™ with Alex Anderson: 24 Designs to Mix
  and Match,* Alex Anderson

Snowflakes & Quilts, Paula Nadelstern

Six Color World: Color, Cloth, Quilts & Wearables,
  Yvonne Porcella

Soft-Edge Piecing, Jinny Beyer

Stitch 'n Flip Quilts: 14 Fantastic Projects, Valori Wells

Wild Birds: Designs for Appliqué & Quilting, Carol Armstrong

Wildflowers: Designs for Appliqué & Quilting,
  Carol Armstrong

For more information write for a free catalog:
C&T Publishing, Inc.
P.O. Box 1456
Lafayette, CA 94549
(800) 284-1114
e-mail: ctinfo@ctpub.com
website: www.ctpub.com

ABOUT THE AUTHOR

Australian textile artist Kristen Dibbs has qualifications in Primary school teaching and Art Education, and has taught adults since 1969. Kristen discovered textile art in 1986, and began teaching her innovative approach to machine embroidery in 1987.

Kristen now presents workshops throughout Australia and New Zealand, and has lectured in Switzerland, USA and Canada. Her magazine articles and three books about machine embroidery have reached an international audience.

Kristen's embroidered artworks are included in private and corporate collections in Australia and overseas. Two examples of her original techniques for embroidered lace work are held in the Powerhouse Museum of Applied Arts in Sydney.

Kristen lives in Sydney with her husband, and divides her time between exploring new techniques with her sewing machine, teaching and writing about machine embroidery and textile arts, and conducting art classes for children.

INDEX